Called To Praise

Ethel Diggs

Called To Praise

Copyright © 2012 by Ethel Diggs

ISBN: 978-0615560878

This book is dedicated to the Worship Team, of Aberdeen Christian Fellowship. Your service has not gone un-noticed, and you all are loved and prayed for.

Acknowledgments

Most of all I would like to thank my Jesus for the inspiration to encourage others in the faith.

I would like to thank Mrs. Brenda Hall for editing and her words of encouragement. Brenda it was a great privilege to work with you.

Last, but not least, I want to thank Mr. Lawrence Diggs for the book design. Lawrence you have been such a wonderful source of encouragement, thank you.

Foreword

Greetings friends, in the name our Lord and Savior Jesus Christ. If He is not your Savior, please make Him your Savior today. You can refer to the prayer on chapter 34 to do this. Please e-mail us about your prayer at singjoy3@net.zero.com.

Singjoy Gospel Ministries has produced the second edition of this devotional "Called to Praise" to edify the body of Christ and minister to those who do not know Him. We pray these devotional thoughts will bless your lives.

Please feel free to contact us with your comments at the e-mail address above.

May God richly bless all who are touched by this message.

Ethel Diggs
First Edition 1992

Second Edition 2011

Called to Praise

Table of Contents

REJOICE AND BE GLAD

"This is the day which the Lord has made; we will be glad and rejoice in it" (*Ps.118:24* KJV).

As a person who has by God's sovereign will and grace, survived suicide, actually being dead for a recorded 30 minutes, I really appreciate this Scripture. I can remember days when I didn't want to live another day. I was not glad for the day or anything else. There are many reasons why people think a day is not good. We as Christians unfortunately are no different. All too often we forget to thank God and appreciate Him just because we got up this morning.

Well, we should be glad just because we serve and have been redeemed by a risen Savior! Even though the psalmist David went through many trials, he had the right idea. He was sought out to be killed and he failed many times; adultery and murder to name a couple of them. Yet he had the right idea. Praising God was always the first order of the day. The psalmist exhorts us to rejoice and be glad in several passages.

Let us take a look at what we have to be glad about. As we notice in the first reference, in this day we can be glad because God made it. We can also be glad that God has given us another day to bring a soul or souls unto Himself. We can be glad that we are another day closer to His coming. We can be glad that we have been chosen from the foundation of the earth, you and I, to fulfill His plan on this day! Hallelujah!!!

So now let us be glad, and put on a happy face. We should be smiling. Others should see on our faces the joy of Jesus. We should be astonishing the world with the "peace that passeth all understanding." Having been employed in sales, I can tell you--we cannot give something away with a smirk or frown on our faces. However, if we are smiling, it is contagious and someone will want to know what makes us so happy! I have found my smile to be my best tool for witnessing. Smiles draw people to me. I do not need to seek them out.

Now, to be glad is not enough. We need to be able to rejoice. If our souls are rejoicing on the inside, it shows on our faces. It shows in how we treat people we come in contact with. It shows in how we conduct our daily lives and handle the details. When the phrase, "Don't worry, be happy," was introduced, I knew the only people who could truly say it and know the meaning, because of their provision, would be Christians.

So join me in making a covenant with God to every single day, rejoice and be glad. "Don't worry, be happy!"

LET US SING PRAISES TO THE MOST HIGH

"I will rejoice in You and be in high spirits; I will sing praise to Your name, O Most High!" (*Psalms 9:2 AMP*)   "I will praise Thee O Lord with my whole heart; I will shew forth thy marvelous works." (*KJV*)

Who is "Thee?" Even more important who is "Thee" to you? As I go about my daily life in everything I do, I am, I see and I need, I am learning more and more everything is of Thee and by Thee. There is absolutely nothing going on in the world that God does not have control over. For all things are of God. I find it incredible that we as human beings think that we have something to do with the involuntary motion of blinking our eyes, daily details, and everything else in our lives and in our world.

Now I wonder, is this a reason to be glad? As we learn the meaning of life through the Scriptures, we learn we can lay our burdens on Him and rest (*Matt 11:28 KJV*). Is this a reason to rejoice? He will never leave us or walk out on us when the going gets tough (*Heb 13:5b KJV*). Is this a reason to sing? What do we require to make us thankful and to make our hearts rejoice? Trust me. Stuff or people will not get the job done. The reality is that stuff is the distraction from the reality of life. He is the way, the truth and the life. (*John 14:6*) When our eyes are on people, they will not be on Jesus, and we will sink into the pit of despair. *(Matt. 14:30)*

I will be glad because God loves me with an everlasting love, and has given me everlasting consolation and good hope through grace to comfort my heart (*II Thessalonians. 2:16-17*). My spirit rejoices in God my Savior, (*Luke 1:47*), my life, and my reality *(Colossians 3:4)*!

I will sing songs of praise and worship to the only One who is worthy. I invite you to join me in rejoicing and singing to the Lord of our Salvation!

WE ARE WHAT WE EAT

"Make me to hear joy and gladness, that the bones which Thou hast broken may rejoice" *(Psalms 51:8KJV)*.

Once I heard a message where the pastor described the work of a shepherd. At a certain point in his illustration he described the sheep that insisted on going too close to the edge of the cliff. Several times the shepherd would take the hook of his staff, hook it around the neck of the sheep and draw it back to the fold. Sometimes as the illustration proceeded, the sheep was persistent about wandering off. It then became necessary for the shepherd to take measures of correction. The shepherd would then break the legs of the sheep. Now the only way the sheep could get around would be on the shoulders of the shepherd.

Then more recently I heard a message preached by my own pastor that ministered the same kind of conviction that the shepherd's staff had ministered to the legs of the sheep. As the song writer said in his song "the joy I hear falling on my ear," this is the grace of our Lord *(Psalms 84:11)*. It is the joy of repent and rebound *(Revelation 2:5)*, and the joy of God's love for me anyway (II Cor. 5:25 *KJV* and *Acts 10:33 KJV*). Our life is in our daily intake of God's Word through categories of doctrine, that is doctrine for every category of our lives *(Romans 6:17 KJV)*. We are what we eat!

REJOICE IN ADVERSITIES

"I will be glad and rejoice in Thy mercy: for Thou hast considered my trouble; Thou has known my soul in adversities" (*Psalms 31:7 KJV*).

Who are we that God is mindful of us (*Psalms 8:4*)? Who am I that God would hear the cry of my sore vexed soul in adversity (*Psalms 6:3*)? Who am I that in the time of trouble He wants to be a place of refuge (*Psalms 9:9*), and deliver me from trouble (*Proverbs 11:8*)? God loves us so much that He does not stop there, but goodness and mercy purges iniquity from us (*Proverbs 16:6*), and because we have received mercy, we faint not (*II Corinthians 4:1*). Well, this is all good news. This is the glorious gospel!

So then, why are we frowning instead of smiling? Why are we complaining and not rejoicing? There is never a season that we should allow rejoicing to cease. A song of praise and thanksgiving should always be on our lips. Consider this, the one thing satan does not want us to do is sing. So the more adversity, the louder we should sing. Singing praises to the Lord is painful to satan's ears. It is the one thing he cannot stand. So let us continue to build ourselves up in Psalms, hymns, and spiritual songs.

REJOICE AND
AGAIN I SAY REJOICE

"Be glad in the Lord and rejoice, ye righteous and shout for joy all ye that are upright in heart" (*Psalms 32:11 KJV*)

We are by faith through grace righteous. We are justified by faith (*Romans 3*). Do we really have a clue of what this means? Do we really know with everything within us that we are in the position of righteousness forever? Is our justification a reality to us in our experience? Our pastors preach and teach daily all these principals, yet on our faces is gloom; and in our emotions we are frustrated, frantic and/or depressed. We seem totally cut off from the truths we are being taught so fervently and diligently. If we are indeed righteous, we are seekers of the righteousness of God. Hence we are truly blessed (*Matthew 5:6*). Jesus tells us this Himself. Thus we are compelled to be glad, for we have the gift of righteousness (*Romans 5:18*) through the blood of Jesus Christ.

We can rejoice because by the grace of almighty God our righteousness is eternal, (*Romans 5:21*). We who have an upright heart (*Proverbs 2:21*), we who experience God's righteousness (upper righteousness) in our daily walk, have reason to shout it out! We will be eager to shout, for the joy of the Lord is our strength (*Nehemiah 8:10*). We can rejoice with joy unspeakable (*I Peter 1:8*). "Rejoice in the Lord always and again I say rejoice (*Philippians 4:4 KJV*)"!

REJOICE SERVE AND TREMBLE

"Serve the Lord with fear, rejoice with trembling."(*Psalms 2:11kjv*).

Fear the Lord, and serve Him in sincerity and truth. To paraphrase: put away our affections for popularity things, power, prestige, riches and traditions, and serve the Lord *(*Joshua 24:14 *kjv*). "Fear the Lord, and serve Him in truth with all your heart" *(*I Samuel 12:24a kjv*). God wants our whole heart. He does not honor half-hearted service as shown in the story of Cain and Abel. We cannot get by with half-hearted service, only giving God the leftovers. Because He lives in our hearts, He is already there to receive what is justly His. So, how and why do we pass our precious Savior by for the affections of our gods, and as an afterthought bring God the leftovers? Consider how great the things He hath done for you (*I Samuel 12:24b kjv*)! If we really considered all the things the Lord has done for us, would we pass Him by for earthly things? I am reminded of the words in the Larnell Harris song, "I would have passed Him by again, but I clearly heard Him say, I miss my time with you".

Jesus says to us in (*John 12:26 kjv*) that if we serve Him, we should follow Him, and where He is we will be, and His Father will honor us. We really miss out when we render service to other than the Lord Jesus Christ. To be honored by God is the maximum, highest praise.

Paul testifies in (*Romans 1:*9 kjv*) that God was his witness that he served with his spirit the gospel of Jesus Christ. We should rejoice in service. Let us have grace whereby we may serve God acceptably with reverence and godly fear. Let us serve Him day and night in fear *(Revelation 7:15)* and trembling for "the Lord reigneth, let the people tremble" *(Psalms 99:1 kjv*). Because Christ lives in our hearts we are always in the presence of God. Will we continue with our attitude of familiarity with the presence of God? Will we not tremble at His Holy presence which "have placed the sand for the bound of the sea by a perpetual decree" *(Jeremiah 5:22 kjv*). "Therefore, hear the word of the Lord, ye that tremble at His Word" *(Isaiah 66:5 kjv*).

REJOICE IN THE FINDS
OF OUR TREASURE HUNT

"Let all those who seek Thee rejoice and be glad in Thee; Let such as love Thy salvation say continually: The Lord be magnified." *Psalms 40:16 KJV*

"I love them that love me, and those that seek Me early shall find me" (*Proverbs 8:17 KJV*). This is certainly reason to rejoice and be glad! If we are not happy, glad, and do not easily and eagerly find reason and time to rejoice, perhaps we are not seekers of God. The scripture has said if we seek Him we find love. Is this not reason to rejoice and be glad? Are we seeking the wisdom of God *(James 1:5)*? Are we desiring God with our whole soul *(Isaiah 26:9)*? Are we seeking first the kingdom of heaven *(Matthew 6:33)* for every situation in our lives? This is a **treasure hunt** and the treasures of God are many! What happens at the end of a treasure hunt? We have found the treasure and there is much gladness and rejoicing!

"And it shall be said in that day; Lo this is our God; We have waited for Him, we will be glad and rejoice in His salvation" *(Isaiah25:9 KJV)*, saying "For I am not ashamed of the gospel of Christ for it is the power of God unto salvation" (*Romans 1:16 KJV*).

Therefore, "O magnify the Lord with me and let us exalt His name together" *(Psalms 34:3 KJV)*.

IN THE GRAVE
WHO SHALL GIVE THEE THANKS

"Rejoice in the Lord ye righteous and give thanks at the remembrance of His holiness" (*Psalms 97:12 KJV*).

We the righteous can rejoice because our righteousness does not depend on us. God is our righteousness and He will bless us by putting a shield around us *(Psalms 5:12)*. Well this set of Scriptures sure blows our excuses for not rejoicing in the Lord! So, if we do not feel holy or righteous we can and must even more rejoice in the righteousness of our God. Our spiritual survival depends on it. "The Lord knoweth the day of the upright; and our inheritance is forever" *(Psalms 37:18 KJV)*. We therefore will march around the church and shout in a loud voice of thanksgiving and tell all the wonderful testimonies of how He has blessed our lives *(Psalms 26:6b)*. Then I will sing (I like this part the best) unto the Lord with all you saints of God and give thanks at the remembrance of His holiness. You see saints, *Psalms 6:5 KJV* says: "For in death there is no remembrance of Thee: in the grave who shall give thanks?"

REJOICING IS
THE ORDER OF THE DAY

"I have set the Lord always before me: because He is at my right hand, I shall not be moved. Therefore my heart is glad and my glory rejoiceth my flesh also shall rest hope" (*Psalms 16:8-9 KJV*).

Now we get to the real reason why there is so much gloom in the body of Christ. Can it be that we always forget to set the Lord before us? Do we forget to acknowledge Him in every aspect of our lives so He can direct us *(Proverbs 3:6)*? Then how can we know that the Lord is on our right hand? Is it any wonder that so many of us are floundering around like chickens with our heads cut off? "Ians" is "Christians" minus "Christ." I do not know if this is even a word, but I do know that we come up just about as short as this word without the acknowledgement of our Lord Jesus Christ in all of our ways. Did you ever try to drive a car with absolutely no gas? We know in fact we do not go anywhere. Without Christ, what does a heart have to be glad about? I have never yet seen anyone rejoice with sadness. I imagine that we would be quite a comical sight. To glory is to honor, and I have never seen or known anyone who was honored by a countenance of gloom.

So then, we conclude that a heart filled with the Holy Spirit and that consults the Lord Jesus for every phase of life is the heart that is glad. This is the heart that rejoiceth! Then our flesh becomes subject to Holy Spirit and will inhabit safe refuge, the Eternal Hope of Glory. Hence my joyful spirit will spring forth a glad countenance and rejoicing is the order of the day.

Rejoice In
The True Image Of God

"The Lord reigneth; let the earth rejoice; let the multitude of isles be glad thereof" *(Psalms 97:1 KJV)*. "The Lord reigneth let the people tremble" *(*Psalms 99:1a KJV*)*. "Say among the heathen that the Lord reigneth" *(Psalms 96:10a KJV)*.

The Lord rules the earth, the Lord rules the people, and the Lord rules the world. Consider this, whatever and wherever God reigns there is peace, there is love, there is grace and mercy. Well then, why do we have such difficulty in allowing Him to rule our lives completely? Perhaps we really do not believe we receive all these wonderful gifts from God's rule. Maybe we think of God in reality as some parents have portrayed Him. He is just someone who will do something awful to us if we make a mistake, or He only loves us if we do good. It is no wonder we do not allow God to take over our lives.

Friends, we can truly trust God to love us. He will extend mercy that lasts forever. This is the picture we should have of God. It then will be easy for us to trust in this Person and be relaxed. We know it takes someone with capacity far beyond ours to care for us in this manner. Once we realize the "real" God, we are in awe and without reservation we tremble in reverence of His Holy name -- just the sound of His name, not to mention His presence! We then truly have reason to be gleeful, to make merry for every season. Acquiring this attitude and realization about God only requires putting away the man-made image of God. We must whole-heartedly receive the Word of God about Who He is. Thus we can rejoice in the truth of who God really is. We will then have no difficulty allowing Him full reign in every aspect of our lives.

REJOICE IN SONGS OF PRAISE UNTO THE LORD

"The Lord is my strength and my shield; my heart trusted in Him, and I am helped; therefore my heart greatly rejoiceth; and with my song will I praise Him" *(Psalms 28:7 KJV)*.

My security, my might, my power is the Lord Jesus Christ. In other words my strength is maximum and nothing and no one can come against me and win! And praise God He did not stop there. The Lord is also my Shield -- anyone or anything trying to get to me, must go through Him! However, the Lord can only protect the part of us we entrust to His care. So when satan's darts connect with some part of us, it is because we did not choose the Lord as our protection.

Consider the following illustration. In the game of football a helmet, shoulder gear, kneepads and various other gear is used to protect the player depending on the position the player operates in. If any player decides he is superman, and goes out on the field to play without protection, without proper gear, he may very well not live to tell of the experience of what it feels like being hit by a Mack truck!

Every time we choose to make or enter into a decision without the Lord's protection, it is like walking out onto an active football field without proper protection. Go or do without the Lord as our shield and strength and we may commit spiritual suicide. Yet if we but choose to receive His protection, we will be secure and confident. We consider that most of the time those guys that have on proper gear get up and walk away after having been hit by 2000 pounds of dead meat crashing on top of them! Therefore, we will choose the Lord's strength, and shield. Thus we will have a song of praise to sing with rejoicing unto the Lord!

LET THE FRUIT OF OUR LIPS BE PRAISE

"My lips shall greatly rejoice when I sing unto Thee; And my soul which Thou hast redeemed" *(*Psalms 71:23 *KJV)*. "O Lord, open Thou my lips; and my mouth shall show forth Thy Praise" *(Psalms 51:15 KJV)*.

I am convinced and convicted that much of what comes out of my own mouth is not praise. I am considering even as I write that if every word or sound that came out of my mouth was praise to God or building up of the body of Christ, what an effect I, for Christ's sake through the Holy Spirit, could have on the world. I am not for one moment entertaining the thought that I could perfectly do this. However, I am prayerfully considering and desiring to each day, each moment, commit my lips, what comes out of my mouth, to the instruction of the Holy Spirit. This in part begins with being cognizant of being in the presence of God. If someone I revere highly is in my presence, I want them to know I love them and hold them in high esteem. I will eagerly praise him or her even if I am not feeling like it. Does God not deserve the same treatment? Since He lives in us, we are always in His presence! Then we would agree with the Psalmist in Psalms 63:3 KJV: "Because Thy loving-kindness is better than life, my lips shall praise thee" and in Psalms 63:5b KJV "my mouth shall praise thee with joyful lips." Perhaps you will join me in a covenant with God that as we learn His statutes, our lips will utter only praise. Therefore let us offer the sacrifice of praise to God continually, that is the fruit of our lips giving thanks to His name; *(Hebrews 13:15)*.

THE RIGHTEOUS
DOTH SING AND REJOICE

"My lips shall greatly rejoice when I sing unto Thee; and my soul, which Thou has redeemed (*Psalms 71:23 KJV*)."

"I will sing unto the Lord, for He hath triumphed gloriously" (*Exodus 15;1b KJV*). Has God triumphed gloriously over your life? Has He saved you, gloriously redeemed you? This seems reason enough to me to go out among the heathen and sing praises unto the name of the Lord *(II Samuel 22:50 KJV)*. (I Chronicles 16:23KJV) seems to admonish us to "sing unto the Lord all the earth, show forth from day to day His salvation." It seems to me with this exhortation, that we have to be either not saved or from another planet to escape singing and celebrating the Lord's salvation. This makes me realize how wonderful salvation in my own life is. God is so personal of course, and some peoples are given to celebration, such as I am. God is so gracious to give me a life of celebration; a life of singing praises to Him. But it is not just my life, but your life as well! Only God knows who the truly good singers are. I believe if our hearts sing for joy of His redemption, God considers and honors each portion according to the heart. Our heart attitude is what sings as a wonderfully sweet fragrance to the nostrils of God. "In the transgression of an evil man there is a snare." (*Proverbs 29:6b KJV*). Therefore we can sing and rejoice because "I come and I will live in the midst of thee saith the Lord" (Zechariah 3:10b KJV).

OUR REDEEMER
IS WORTHY OF PRAISE

"My lips shall greatly rejoice when I sing unto Thee; And my soul, which Thou hast redeemed" (*Psalms 71:23* KJV).

"The law of the Lord is perfect converting the soul" (*Psalms 19:7a* KJV). Our conversion is the perfect law, plan, and will of God. Yet after we are saved we often do not allow God's conversion. It reminds me of taking a bath after jogging ten miles and then putting the same clothes back on. Just imagine this, and then maybe God will be allowed to do as He wills in our lives. God gave us free volition, which permitted us to think. Thus we think we know best for us; better than God. However, that brings us to His next point the "testimony of the Lord is sure, making wise the simple." Maybe if we stop being so smart, God's wisdom will replace what we think we know. (Psalms 34:22KJV) says "The Lord redeemeth the soul of His servant, and none of them that trust in Him shall be desolate." He plans is to take care of us as soon as we allow Him to. Christ has redeemed us from the curse of the law, being made a curse for us: "For it is written; cursed is everyone that hangeth from a tree" (*Galatians 3:13* KJV).

Christ did not go through all this to help us just be redeemed, but in fact paid in full the ransom for our sin. In conclusion we can sing a new song, saying "Thou art worthy to take the book and open the seals thereof: for Thou wast slain and hast redeemed us to God by Thy blood out of every kindred, and tongue and people, and nation and hast made us unto our God kings and priest; and we shall reign on the earth" (*Revelation 5:9-10* KJV).

LET US GO FORTH IN PRAISE

"We will rejoice in Thy salvation and in the name of our God we will set up our banners; The Lord fulfill all thy petitions." (*Psalms 20:5* KJV)

Lord, we will make known to the world with merry making that You have delivered us! You have redeemed us from the curse, from death. You have delivered us out of the darkness of sin before we loved You and acknowledged You. We will give thanks in the presence of the heathens, Your enemies. We will be faithful to glorify Your name in all things. You are our God so we will hoist the flag high to announce our allegiance to You. You have honored and fulfilled all our requests. So then, we will praise you without ceasing.

What a commitment! What a prayer and covenant to make with God. Are we willing to commit, to spend our lives praising God? Or would it take too much time away from complaining, being absorbed by daily details, and living in frustration from reacting in our own flesh to deal with it.

Consider this, if we were spending our time praising God we would then be able to live in the experience of "in whatever state I am, therewith to be content" (*Philippians 4:11b* KJV). Thus we would then have the peace of God, which passeth all understanding (*Philippians 4:7* KJV) and our hearts and mind would be kept through Christ Jesus (*Phillipians4:7 b* KJV) .

LET US CONSIDER
THE HOLINESS OF OUR GOD

"God hath spoken in His holiness; I will rejoice" (*Psalms 60:6a* KJV).

Let us consider the holiness of our God. Do we, and can we by a stretch of our finite minds perceive the holiness of God? "Who is like unto Thee, O Lord among the gods? Who is like Thee, glorious in holiness, fearful in praises, doing wonders" (*Exodus 15:11* KJV). Can we find anyone or anything to compare to God and/or His holiness? Yet it is obvious that we try. "Give unto the Lord the glory due unto His name, bring offerings and come before Him; Worship the Lord in the beauty of holiness" (*I Chronicles 16:29* KJV). If we do not practice being in His presence we will miss the glorious experience of Him, thereby never getting to know the God we serve. It seems to me the easiest way to live cognitive of His presence is to continually praise Him. "Sing unto the Lord, O ye saints of His, and give thanks at the remembrance of His holiness" (*Psalms 30:4* KJV). How could we forget His holiness if we are in continuous praise, for the Lord inhabits our praise!

THE PROTECTION OF HIS WINGS

"Because thou hast been my help, therefore in the shadows of Thy wings I rejoice" (*Psalms 63:7* KJV).

God is our refuge and strength, a very present help in trouble (*Psalms 46:1*KJV). There is no need to be consumed in daily details, trials, or anything else. He is presently here for us, not to help; He is THE help. He will redeem us for His mercies' sake (*Psalms 44:26*). We say as the Psalmist, "But I am poor and needy." Then we must also realize that "yet the Lord thinketh upon me." He is watching us and watching out for us. Because in our tiny frame of reference we cannot even imagine the control God has over everything we sweat. We only need ask, to say, "Thou art my help and my deliverer." I was quite amused while studying in finding how many times the Psalmist said "hurry up God!" He was always saying "make haste God." In this particular scripture he says; "make no tarrying O my God" (*Psalms 40:17*KJV). Don't you just love it when God takes our support system? You know those times we seem to be friendless—the times when we come to grips with, "Unless the Lord had been my help, my soul had almost dwelt in silence" (*Psalms94:17* KJV). This is why it is of utmost importance to praise our God—to make praise a state of continuance of our whole being.

We have shelter in the shadow of His wings. If we can grasp (as the Psalmist did) how much God loves us, we can say to the Lord, "Keep me as the apple of the eye, hide me under the shadow of Thy wings" (*Psalms 17:8* KJV). Here we can put our trust because, there is protection in the shadow His wings. His loving kindness is excellent. So He gives us a place to hide when calamities strike. If there is a heavy downpour of rain and you get caught unexpectedly, when you find cover you give a huge sigh of relief and some exclamation of praise. So then rejoice in the much, needed, covering of the Lord's grace, mercy, peace, and love!

THE LITTLE HILLS REJOICE ON EVERY SIDE

"Thou crownest the year with Thy goodness; and Thy paths drop fatness. They drop upon the pastures of the wilderness; and the little hills rejoice on every side" (*Psalms 65:11-12*KJV).

Take a look around us, what do you see? Are we living outside in a park? Are we suffering from malnutrition, exposure of the elements? Or rather has the Lord served us with fatness? There are those of us who insist on being in the open fields, hanging out in the elements. Have you ever been the parent or overseer of a two-year-old child? The general disposition of a two year old is "what can I do next to push this big person's button" and they are very fast and steady. Most adults I know, including myself, after a while would be ready to bring our wrath to the bottom of that particular child. Yet, while we flirt with the world's system, play church, and exhibit familiar attitudes towards our Savior, God drops fatness in our houses. What is our attitude when life starts falling apart? Do we seek God's face or do we grumble? We want to know why God will not fix this or that and "can God furnish a table in the wilderness?" (*Psalms78:19b*). Even so God is faithful. As long as we live, we have a chance to come to Him. We can come to the realization that God loves us and we can come to Him saying, "I am like a pelican in the wilderness; I am an owl in the desert."

Some of us get so far out; we become solitary and cannot find our way back to God's house. God loves us so much that He often turns the desert place into a water spring and the rivers into wilderness. Thus, "then shall the lame man leap as a deer, and the tongue of the dumb sing; for in the wilderness shall waters break out and streams in the desert." Thus will, "the little hills" the vessels, the recipients of God's grace, rejoice on every side.

HAVE A PARTY FOR JESUS

"But let the righteous be glad; let them rejoice before God: yea, let them exceedingly rejoice" (*Psalms 68:3*KJV).

Let the saints of God be happy! Let those who love the Lord and all His precepts be joyful. Oh, I know! Let all Christians have a party! Yes, trust me this is a great idea. Come now and join me, you can help me with the plans. Maybe you will make a list of other guests. Since our pastors are masters at feeding us, we should have them prepare the feast. After all He is our betrothed, we must have the very best of everything. Now then, the best people to serve the feast are the elders and deacons. I think the missionaries would be the most likely to have conversation that would interest the Lord. We'll have a huge choir and orchestra, and mimes, and so forth. Does this sound a bit like heaven? This is the picture I want to portray. This state of being is not so far-fetched. If we live in a constant attitude of praise our lives can take on this heavenly activity. Praising God is the life! You can count on a visit often from the Holy Spirit. If you want to draw close to the Lord, just start praising Him. God inhabits our praise and we will surely get to know His presence intimately by living in a constant state of praise.

PRAISE TO THE GOD OF MERCY

"O satisfy us early with thy mercy; that we may rejoice and be glad all our days" (*Psalms 90:14*KJV).

Have you ever witnessed a sunrise, or a waterfall, or a flower blooming in early spring? Have you witnessed the birth of a child, or small children playing, or how about a school of whales migrating or a flock of geese?

Most of these activities happen early in the morning. It seems to me that nature has the right idea. I have had occasion to be up and out early in the morning and there is just something about this time that draws me into praise. It seems all evidence of God's presence is right in front of me. His loving-kindness is not obscured by daily details. He is right there out in the open to love and to be loved, to touch and to be touched. The days when I can have the opportunity to meet God in this place are the most wonderful and memorable times I have spent with the Lord. They remind me of the scripture in I Peter 1:8 "joy unspeakable". These are the times that speak the reality of who God is, and I am bathed in His mercy and love to ultimate satisfaction.

Nothing breaks me out in a smile quicker than the handiwork of my Creator. He is truly awesome and worthy of all praise. God is the only awesome God. I am truly glad and my heart leaps within me.

Praise to the God of mercy.

REJOICING STOPS POLLUTION

"The righteous shall see it, and rejoice: and all iniquity shall stop her mouth." (*Psalms 107:42* KJV)

Do we believe that praise and rejoicing in the works of the Lord can stop the mouth of iniquity? Much of the attitude in the world about God comes from the church. Each of us represents the church. Let me illustrate.

How many of us run to the world's system to settle grievances against each other? Yes we get bold when some of us even resort to taking God's church to court. How about those of us who resort to the world system's psychology to deal with what usually results in decisions contrary to God's plan for our lives? What about more subtle incidents like being familiar with each other, or a fellow worker [not letting our light shine], or being familiar with the pulpit? Please do not feel that I am pointing a finger. I only know about most of these from being convicted by the Holy Spirit in my own life. Praise God I have repented and this will certainly serve to remind me of God's grace and love towards me.

This is the point I want to make. If my heart is one of rejoicing because all my sins are paid for in full, and if I am rejoicing even in the face of adversity; iniquity has absolutely nothing to feed on. There is no negativity in the atmosphere that comes from me. You see I understand that every time I speak negativity into the atmosphere it causes spiritual pollution that may prevent someone from coming to the saving knowledge of Christ—that someone's blood may be required at my hand [I am using first person here because I realize this is strong].

Just think of this: our rejoicing, merry making, and praising the Lord will shut the mouth, bridle the tongue, and snuff out the lies of iniquity.

REJOICING IN OUR TABERNACLES

"The voice of rejoicing and salvation is in the tabernacle of the righteous; the right hand of the Lord doeth valiantly." (*Psalms118:15*KJV)

The joyous proclamation of deliverance is in the house of the righteous. Somehow I do not think we have to go t church to praise the Lord. This scripture is saying that this sound, this declaration of salvation is in our house; in our bodies. Maybe just our presence should shout out the fact Jesus is Lord. When someone visits your home do you have to hide things or run to turn off the TV or change the station on the radio? Do we dress one way to go to church, and another to go other places?

What I am trying to say is that everything we do should praise God. Everything in our lives should out our deliverances. I just realized that I keep going on about this proclamation of salvation. Maybe you are reading this and you do not have salvation. Well I want you to know and have Jesus, so you can shout it out.

Let me tell you this; "for by grace ye are saved, through faith; and that not of yourselves; it is a gift of God" (*Ephesians 2:8*KJV). "If thou shalt confess with the Lord Jesus and shalt believe in thine heart that God has raised Him from the dead, thou shalt be saved" (*Romans 10:9*KJV). And "neither is there salvation in any other: for there is none other name under heaven given among men, whereby we must be saved" (*Acts 4:12*KJV).

Now then, let us pray together saying, **"Yes Lord, I believe that you were raised from the dead, and believing on the name of Jesus is the only way I can be saved. I am a sinner and I need to be saved more than I need anything on the face of the earth. Lord Jesus, please come into my heart and change my life. Thank You Jesus, for saving my soul. In Jesus' name, thank You God. Amen."** Now please join us in this joyous proclamation of deliverance! Let this proclamation be on the lips of every believer; "for the right hand of the Lord doeth valiantly."

Declare His Works With Rejoicing

"And let them sacrifice the sacrifices of thanksgiving and declare His works with rejoicings." (*Psalm 107:22*KJV)

God gave us the ultimate example of sacrifice, when He gave us His Son; the sacrifice of sacrifices. He does not require us to literally go on a cross, but our love for Him should compel us to be willing. Love requires the sacrifice of fully trusting Him; the sacrifice of joy *(Psalms 27:6)*, the sacrifice of righteousness *(Psalms 51:19)*, and let us present our bodies as a living sacrifice *(Romans 12:1)*.

This means that all of my rights, ambitions, esteem and ego are taken to the cross, thus I am totally emptied out to be filled with the Holy Spirit. Then only what is of God is fit for my participation. Therefore, every morning when I pick up my hot cup of new mercies, I empty my flesh on the altar of the cross, hence becoming a new creation every single day.

I heard my pastor say on more than one occasion that we must everyday "on purpose" acknowledge our crucifixion. I know in fact if and when I do not practice this, satan just sneaks his ugly head up when I least expect it.

Then there is the sacrifice of praise, which God inhabits. I cannot say this enough. Just think of it, God becomes evident, manifest in our praise. I am more convinced each day this is a way to be intimate with our Savior.

Have you ever had someone do something for you, and you knew there was nothing you could do to thank him or her enough? Well, Jesus died for our sins as a common criminal, and God the Father sent Him. Trust me when I say we cannot thank God the Father, or the Lord Jesus Christ, enough.

So sacrifice the sacrifices of thanksgiving and declare His works.

THE GOLDEN BRICK

"Thy testimonies have I taken as a heritage forever: for they are the rejoicing of the heart." (*Psalms 119:111*KJV)

Our path is lighted by the Word of God, and we get understanding from His precepts, and meditate on His sayings. What God has to say is so sure that our houses become holy. This should be of great comfort to us, since we live in a system of broken contracts, promises and false testimonies. People always change their minds about what they want, who they are, and who they think we are. God's Word never changes, because He never changes. Heaven and earth shall pass away, but the Word of God never fails. This is the key part of our godly inheritance, for without the Word of God we would have no guide to our ultimate heritage, eternal life. There would be no way for us to know we have a heritage if God had not inspired His Word to be written.

The next time you pick up your Bible, consider that it is more valuable than a pure gold brick its size. However, the gold brick has been wrapped to be protected. If we do not take the wrapper off, we will not know how rich we really are. Thus we have much reason for rejoicing whether we hear, read or sing the Word of God.

NOTHING FROM NOTHING
EQUALS WEEDS

"He that goeth forth and weepeth, bearing seed for sowing, shall doubtless come again with rejoicing, bringing his sheaves with him." (*Psalms126:6* KJV)

How will we eat bread if we sow no seed for the wheat? What good is it that we are rich in many acres of fertile land, and we just let it sit there? We even brag about our beautiful land and how rich the soil is. In reality we are only repeating what the person that sold the land to us had said. You see, since we have not planted any seed, we do not know the reality of the richness of our land. Even more tragic, we have seed we have bought every time we have gone to market, and we just store it. As a matter of fact, wasn't there some strange weed coming out of those seed sacks? Then we become frustrated when we look all around us and everybody else has beautiful fields of grain being ripened to harvest. Since we sleep in and watch TV, or hang out at the mall, we never see what the others do. We missed the early morning planting, and of course our favorite TV show was on when our neighbor was watering and pulling weeds.

Now isn't it pitiful that God has made our hearts rich and fertile soil, and when we go to church the pastor pours into the sack the best seed there is, and yet we have nothing to show for it.

Who have you shared your faith with lately, what the Lord has done for you? Did you not hear a soul-shaking message on Sunday or Wednesday? What are you doing with your seeds? Seeds stored in a bag somewhere cannot produce fruit. The seed we are bearing is precious seed and if we go all out planting and watering with our tears, we shall doubtless come again with rejoicing and bringing in our sheaves with us.

Make A Joyful Noise And Bury The Devil

"Make a joyful noise unto the Lord, all the earth; make a loud noise and rejoice and sing praise." (*Psalms 98:4* KJV)

Well, let us get ready to make a statement. Let us put away all of our inhibitions and preconceived notions about how we think we are supposed to praise. Where I come from, we would say, let's have a hallelujah break down. Let us act like we are at our favorite sporting event. Don't laugh; we make more noise for man's sake than to the glory of God. Well I know some of us will never be able to do this, after all it isn't dignified. However, I did not make up this verse. I really think that there should be at least sometimes enough noise to knock down the walls. Is it not true that the noise of the shouts brought down the walls of Jericho? When the noise is joyful, can we imagine how many demons would go flying? Listen, a joyful noise serves notice to the defeat of satan.

Can you imagine what it would be like if the body of Christ all over the world at the same time let off a huge loud round of praise? I get goose bumps just thinking about it. I think something like this would serve as what we call in the rodeo a rope and tie. It would be something like this; everyone in the body of Christ would together at the same time, all over the world and give a Jericho shout. I think it would be so intense that satan and his crew would be chased to the deepest part of hell. Then as long as we could keep the intensity going, satan and his crew would be tied up in hell. Well, this isn't so far fetched because when we praise God, it does send satan right up over the wall; satan hates it even more when you sing. If you are going through something, start singing. Praise God in every season and rejoice on every hand.

We as Christians are the only people on the face of the earth that have a bona fide reason to be joyful; rejoice, and praise the living God.

COMPLETE TRUST IN GOD YIELDS A REJOICING HEART

"For our heart shall rejoice in Him, because we trusted in His Holy name." (*Psalms 33:21* KJV)

Who or what are we putting our trust in? Most of us will answer; my trust is in the Lord. However, if we took a moment-by-moment inventory of our lives, that may not be the case at all. It is my conviction, that what controls our lives are things and even people where our trust is vested. Do we make plans, and then ask God to go along with the program, or do we ask God to show us what His plan is for our walk is each day?

Each day as we release more of ourselves to the Lord Jesus, we will find our lives taking unimaginable changes. God can then do things with and through us that we think we can only dream of. God really wants to use all of us in His own special, unique, for each of us plans. It only requires that we step up from the position of pride. We only need to realize that God is the power by which everything moves, including us. Thus, even if we are in adverse circumstances, we will be at peace. I think that I am finally learning that if I am anxious or upset about how life is going, I have then, as pastor says it, "usurped the authority of God" in the situation and there will not be peace until God is in full power of it. Remember, God will not violate our free volition. We need to decide to have peace by turning it over to God. Only our trust in God completely will yield a rejoicing heart.

GOD GETS THE LAST LAUGH

"I will extol the, O Lord; for Thou hast lifted me up. And not made my foes to rejoice over me." (*Psalms 30:1* KJV)

Has something or someone come against you lately? This verse should be a great consolation for us. The good news does not stop there. Stay with me and be excited about God in your life, the daily details, or monstrosities. "The Lord is our light and our salvation" (*Psalms 27:1a* KJV). He is just waiting to deliver us. "Whom shall I fear" (*Psalms 27:1b* KJV). My dad taught me at a very young age, "If it ain't bigger than God, you ain't got to be scared of it." I would say that is wisdom, and these words have carried me places. "The Lord is the strength of my life" (*Psalms 27:1c* KJV). A pastor friend of mine was instructing me in how to obtain bookings for singing engagements. He said, "If you want help you have to be helpless, you need to ask for help" (more words of wisdom).

You see, we often do not get help from God because we have our own strength. We have the attitude; "just stand aside God, I can do this myself." We are like an illustration I heard in a message: There was a young boy out playing. He came to a large rock that he thought he wanted to add to his collection. He needed to move the rock because it was wedged. He struggled for a considerable amount of time. Standing near by watching all this time was the boy's father. The child in frustration and disappointment gave up his struggle.

Finally the father said to his son, "Have you done everything you can to obtain your rock?"

The boy answered, "Yes, and I cannot budge it."

Well the father asked the boy this question several times. The boy became exasperated with the question as well.

Then his father said, "Son I have been standing here waiting for you to ask for help.".

"When the wicked, even mine enemies and my foes, come upon me to eat my flesh, they stumbled and fell" (*Psalms 27:2* KJV).

So, do not worry about who gets after you, because they are not bigger than God, and God will lift us up. He gets the praise, the glory, and the last laugh!

REHEARSAL FOR ETERNAL PRAISE

"Rejoice evermore." (*I Thessalonians 5:16* KJV)

"And thou shalt rejoice in every good thing which the Lord thy God hath given unto thee, and unto thine house, thou and the Levite, and the stranger that is among you" (Deuteronomy 26:11 KJV).

I take from this verse that God wants us to make such a fuss about everything He does that it would be contagious to whoever is around us. And "thou shalt rejoice in thy feast, thou and thy maidservant, and the Levite, and the stranger, and the fatherless, and the widow that are within thy gates" (Deuteronomy 16:14 KJV).

So we should bless the Lord in rejoicing at the time we eat, everyone who eats with us should rejoice. Can you imagine eating at a restaurant and causing the whole place to go into holy rejoicing? Well I love the thought of it and some day….

"Now therefore arise, O Lord God, into Thy resting place, Thou and the ark of Thy strength: let Thy saints rejoice in goodness" (II Chronicles 6:41 KJV). Is God good to you? Has He blessed you with a godly pastor? Then rejoice in His goodness!

The list goes on and on. Rejoice at the sound of the organ. Rejoice in His mercy, in His work, and over them that do good.

No matter what we rejoice in there is the one great time and cause to rejoice. We can rejoice in the hope of the glory of God. I suggest we get well practiced, because we are getting ready for eternal rejoicing.

WEEP WITH, PRAY FOR AND LOVE YOUR FRIENDS

"Rejoice with them that do rejoice, and weep with them that weep" (Romans12:15 KJV).

There are a lot of hurting people all over this world. However, It is devastating to see the many hurting people in the body of Christ. I wonder, Lord how can we help to heal others when we are hurting so badly? I have seen illness, depression, anger, and so forth. I think it is very clear when the scripture says to weep with those who weep. Jesus tells us to love one another. When we do love one another, our hearts break to see those whom we love weep, hurt, and suffering.

The idea here is not to become depressed, but to bear one another up, build one another up in the Lord and pray for one another. We really do have the best tools of all people as Christians to help our beloved friends. We have prayer and love. Since everything that means anything hinges on love, God's love for us, and our love for one another. Through prayer and love, those who weep will soon be rejoicing. Thus we can rejoice with them that rejoice.

LET THE BROTHER OF LOW DEGREE REJOICE

"Let the brother of low degree rejoice in that he is exalted; but the rich, in that he is made low" James 1:9 KJV.

How many of us would be depressed if we suddenly had a million dollars? We may see some tears of joy. We might be entered into the world book of records for having the widest smile or even better yet, for praising God the loudest. Somehow, no one would have to remind us that God has been good to us, that is, if we loved God. Now I know we have a very good picture of what we each, on our own would do. However, notice James1:10a, "but the rich in that he is made low." Rejoice if we lose a million dollars. "Yeah right." Hey, it's in the book. The point here is not how much money we have, but who we are with or without it. You see, my friends, only who we are in Christ is eternal.

So we then conclude that we, who can honestly rejoice in being made low, have a greater treasure than money. We can further conclude that since God loves us whether rich or poor, then God's love is the true rejoicing factor. I am convinced that true happiness is freedom from the bondage of the world system. True freedom is to love God and by faith live by every word that proceeds out of the mouth of God. I have been made low and I have truly rejoiced!!!

About the Author

Ms Diggs now lives in South Dakota with her husband Jonathan Nerland. Together they minister in the Lord's work.

If you wish to make comments about this book, you may contact us at singjoy3@netzero.com.

www.ingramcontent.com/pod-product-compliance
Lightning Source LLC
Chambersburg PA
CBHW030308030426
42337CB00012B/641